D1174512

Emily®

and the Strangers

YOU DON'T HAVE TO BE CUTE TO BE AWSOME!
TONIGHT!
THE STRANGERS
HELP THE KITTIES!
THE STRANGERS
NOW IN DULLSVILLE!
ONE NIGHT ONLY
THE STRANGERS
THE STRANGERS
STRANGE OUT!

Emily® and the Strangers

Volume 3
ROAD TO NOWHERE TOUR

Created by
ROB REGER

Written by
MARIAH HUEHNER
and **ROB REGER**

Art by
CAT FARRIS

Lettering by
NATE PIEKOS of **BLAMBOT®**

Cover art by
CAT FARRIS and **BUZZ PARKER**

Endpaper art by
EMILY IVIE

DARK HORSE BOOKS

Mike Richardson

Editors Katii O'Brien
and Hannah Means-Shannon

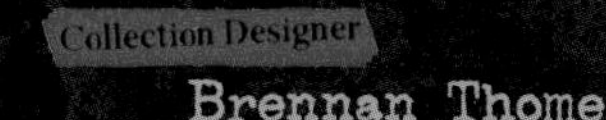

Brennan Thome

Digital Art Technician

Allyson Haller

Flats by Gabe Fischer

Special thanks to
Jim Gibbons and Scott Allie.

Published by Dark Horse Books
A division of Dark Horse Comics, Inc.
10956 SE Main Street
Milwaukie, OR 97222

First edition: March 2017
ISBN 978-1-50670-058-8

1 3 5 7 9 10 8 6 4 2
Printed in China

Advertising Sales: (503) 905-2237
International Licensing: (503) 905-2377
Comic Shop Locator Service: (888) 266-4226

DarkHorse.com | Facebook.com/DarkHorseComics | Twitter.com/DarkHorseComics

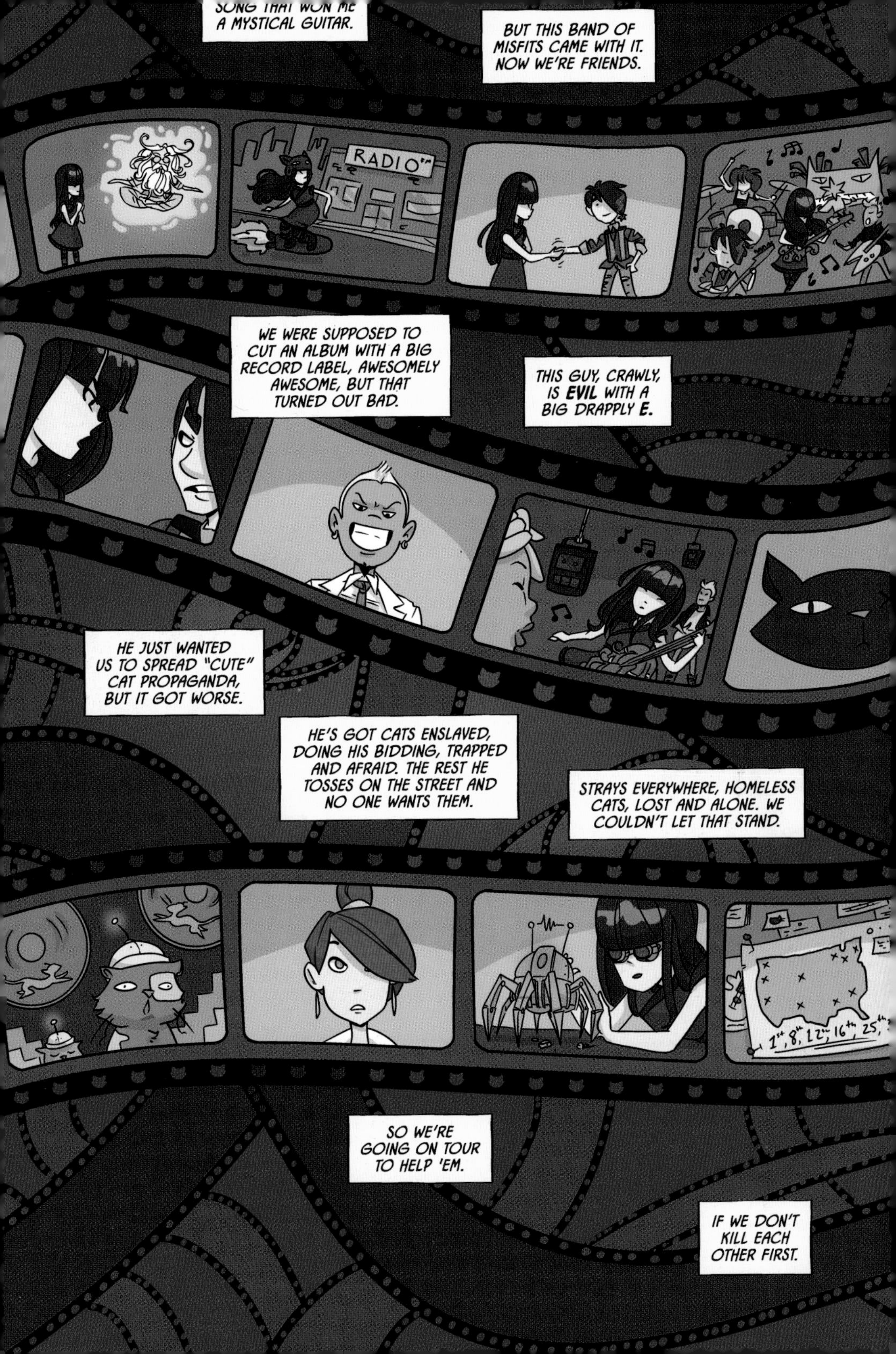
SONG THAT WON ME A MYSTICAL GUITAR.
BUT THIS BAND OF MISFITS CAME WITH IT. NOW WE'RE FRIENDS.
RADIO
WE WERE SUPPOSED TO CUT AN ALBUM WITH A BIG RECORD LABEL, AWESOMELY AWESOME, BUT THAT TURNED OUT BAD.
THIS GUY, CRAWLY, IS **EVIL** WITH A BIG DRAPPLY **E.**
HE JUST WANTED US TO SPREAD "CUTE" CAT PROPAGANDA, BUT IT GOT WORSE.
HE'S GOT CATS ENSLAVED, DOING HIS BIDDING, TRAPPED AND AFRAID. THE REST HE TOSSES ON THE STREET AND NO ONE WANTS THEM.
STRAYS EVERYWHERE, HOMELESS CATS, LOST AND ALONE. WE COULDN'T LET THAT STAND.
SO WE'RE GOING ON TOUR TO HELP 'EM.
IF WE DON'T KILL EACH OTHER FIRST.

HAD TO GET OUT AND CRUISE FOR A WHILE.
TOO CRAMMED UP WITH THE BAND THESE DAYS.
TOO MUCH TO DO. ESPECIALLY WITH THE TOUR LOOMIN' LARGE.
THAT CREEP OF A RECORD LABEL STOOGE CRAWLY'S GOING TO PAY FOR TRYIN' TO MESS WITH ME.
US.
THIS TOUR NEEDS TO BE THE HUCKBATTING **BEST.**
A TOUR LIKE NO OTHER. AND WITH MY INCREDIZORKIN' PLAN? IT WILL BE.
MY FRIENDS.
HEY, EMILY!
WILLOW. RAVEN. TRILOGY! DON'T EAT THAT.
TOUR
NOTHING'S GONNA GO WR--
WE'VE GOT A HUGE PROBLEM.
NOW WHAT?
PROBABLY NOTHING THAT MAJOR.
HURRY!
BAD WIRE. BAD!

FARDWARKS AND SCUZZLESCUMS!
KUTE KITTY WOW
TOUR: 1ST, 4TH, 8TH, 12TH, 20TH, 22ND
SEE, EMILY?
WE TOLD YOU.
THEY LOOK A LOT LIKE US, ONLY...
DO YOU THINK IT'S...?
CRAWLY? WHO ELSE?
OOOOOH, SHINY!
THEY'RE VERY... CLEAN.
THIS IS ALL ABOUT GETTIN' BACK AT ME FOR TURNING HIM DOWN. FOR NOT SPREADING HIS CRUDDY MESSAGES ABOUT "CUTE" CATS AS THE BEST.
SHE'S NOT AS AWESOME AS YOU...
NO ONE IS.

OBVIOUSLY CRAWLY THINKS HE AND HIS RECORD LABEL CAN STOP OUR TOUR WITH HIS ROCK-BOT BAND. HE THINKS HE CAN STOP US FROM EXPOSING HIS CAPTIVE CAT CORPS.
WELL, HE CAN'T. WE'RE GOING TO DO SOMETHING SO EPIC, SO GARBLOTTINGLY PHENOMENAL, HE'LL BE SORRY HE MESSED WITH US.
OKAY, BUT WHAT ABOUT THE TOUR?
WHEEE!
TRILOGY! GET DOWN!
THE TOUR WILL BE FINE.
WE NEED TO GET BACK AT CRAWLY FOR THIS FIRST.
I DON'T KNOW, EMILY. THIS SEEMS LIKE A... DISTRACTION.
TRILOGY, NO!
I MEAN, DO WE NEED TO PARACHUTE IN WITH TIME-STOPPING JET SKIS?
IT'S THE ONLY WAY TO GET MY BUGABOO BOT BACK. WE NEED ITS INTEL TO STOP CRAWLY.
THAT NEW BAND IS JUST SOME BLATHERCAT COPY OF US. THEY DON'T MATTER.
WE NEED TO TAKE 'EM DOWN FOR MESSING WITH US.
BUGABOO BOT
YEAH, BUT--
WE HAVE THE TOUR AND THE ALBUM. IT'S SUPPOSED TO BE ABOUT HELPING THE CATS, NOT GETTING BACK AT CRAWLY.
WE'RE A BAND. NOT SUPER-HEROES.
YEAH, MY BAND.
SO I SAY WHAT WE DO AND WHERE WE GO, HAIRGEL.
WE'RE ALL IN THIS TOGETHER.
LET'S NOT FIGHT. WE'VE BEEN GETTING ALONG SO WELL...
EMILY, HE'S JUST TRYING TO HELP. HE WORRIES ABOUT YOU--
I'M NOT ARGUING. EVAN IS THE ONE BEING DIFFICULT.

LOOK, EVAN CAN HAVE HIS LITTLE CRUSH ON ME OR WHATEVER. I DON'T CARE.
EXCEPT WHEN IT GETS IN THE WAY.
HE NEEDS TO GET OVER THE SOPPY STUFF.
HEY, MAN, WAIT UP...
I, *UM,* NEED SOME FRESH AIR...
EMILY!
THAT WAS CRUEL AND THOUGHTLESS.
YOU KNOW BETTER THAN THAT.
WHAT?
YOU'RE SO BUSY BEING TOUGH YOU CAN'T TREAT A FRIEND WITH A LITTLE RESPECT?
I'M DISAPPOINTED IN YOU.
I WAS SHOWIN' HIM RESPECT BY NOT MINCING WORDS, BUT...
...MAYBE I COULD HAVE PHRASED IT BETTER.
YOU THINK?
FINE, I'LL DEAL WITH EVAN. BUT LATER. WE HAVE WORK TO DO.

I...HOPE THE FRESH AIR WAS USEFUL. NOW LET'S GET TO IT.
OKAY, BUT WE NEED TO TALK LATER.
SURE. BUT NOW, WE NEED TO INVENT! BUILD! MAKE WITH THE SCIENCE!
SIGH

AWESOMELY AWESOME
CATS
US
WATER BALLOONS
CRAWLY

SO IF WE CAN MAKE THE PARACHUTES INTO TENTS, THEN--
WE DON'T HAVE TIME. WE NEED SOMETHING SIMPLE.

MY PLAN WILL WORK.
MAYBE, BUT IT'LL TAKE TOO LONG TO MAKE EVERYTHING. WE NEED TO GET THIS DONE AND GET TO THE TOUR.

ARE YOU SAYIN' I'M SLOW?
JUST BECAUSE I HAVE CRABSTUNNINGLY AWESOME IDEAS DOES NOT MAKE THEM COMPLICATED.
NO, JUST... YOU GET CARRIED AWAY WITH YOUR IDEAS AND MAKE EVERYTHING COMPLICATED.
IT KINDA DOES...
STOP!
YOU TWO SQUABBLE TOO MUCH.
WE NEED TO GO TO THE ETHER OF SOUND. GET OURSELVES SORTED.
NOW, THINK OF VERY WONDERFUL THINGS LIKE BEES AND ICE CREAM...
YES.
NOW SHUT 'EM!
DO WE HAVE TO HOLD HANDS?
UGH.
CAN YOU FEEL THE BEAT? IT'S LIKE VIOLETS SINGING WITH CHOCOLATE!

HEY, PROFESSA.
WELCOME, STRANGERS, TO THE UTMOST, ULTIMATE, ULULATING ULTRA!
THE CACOPHONONICALLY SPLENDID ETHER AND ITS ***WALL OF SOUND!***
MY TEETH FEEL WEIRD HERE.
RHYTHM RIVER
YEAH, MY EARS ARE SORT OF VIBRATING.
CAREFUL! YOU GET A FOOT IN THE RIVER AND IT'LL SING FOREVER.
SINGING FEET?
BEAT HILLS

SILENCE + NOISE WALL
IT'S LIKE EVERY SOUND I'VE EVER LOVED IS PLAYING ALL AT ONCE...

JUST PLAYING WITH THE BEAT. YOU KNOW HOW IT IS.
WE'RE IN A SCRAPE. AGAIN.
AND I WANT TO MAKE SOMETHING REALLY RAD TO FIX IT BUT--
THEY THINK IT'S TOO COMPLICATED.
HMM. DO YOU HEAR THAT DISHARMONY? LIKE A BUZZ IN YOUR EAR?
KINDA.
WELL, HERE'S HOW YOU NEED TO BREAK IT DOWN...
YOU GOT TO RIDE THE WAVELENGTHS, LET THE SOUNDS DO WHAT THEY WILL.
THE HEART KNOWS THE RHYTHM AND THE RHYTHM CARRIES THE WORD.
UH... WHAT?
HOW... HELPFUL?
THAT WAS TRILOGY-LEVEL VAGUE, MAN.
HE MEANS WE HAVE TO MAKE OUR IDEAS TAKE SHAPE.
INTO SOMETHING CONCRETE AND USEFUL. NOT JUST GADGETS FOR ONE CAPER.
SOMETHING THAT'S ***OURS.***
HERE, WHERE IT'S ALL SOUND, WHERE THOUGHTS AND FEELINGS COME TOGETHER INTO MUSIC...
WE MAKE THE INTANGIBLE...
TANGIBLE.
I...ACTUALLY UNDERSTOOD THAT.
I THINK TRILOGY JUST MADE SENSE.
WOW.

THE LITTLE SYMPHONY HAS IT.
AND THAT MEANS, MY FRIENDS, THAT THIS IS MY FINAL ENCORE.
YOU DON'T NEED ME ANYMORE. AND I'VE GOT HARMONIES TO MAKE.
BUT...WHAT IF WE GET INTO TROUBLE?
YOUR MUSIC BROUGHT US TOGETHER.
YOU NEED EACH OTHER MORE THAN YOU EVER NEEDED ME.
JUST REMEMBER THE SOUNDS AND YOU'LL BE OKAY.
THANK YOU.
HONORED, LITTLE INVENTOR. NOW DON'T FORGET TO PLAY!
BYE, PROFESSA.

THAT'S... NOT WHAT I WAS EXPECTING.
I THINK IT MIGHT BE A LITERAL BUCKET OF BOLTS...

IF WE BUILD IT, THE CATS WILL COME.
I WANT BLUE ICE CREAM!
WELL, TRILOGY'S SANITY STREAK DIDN'T LAST LONG.

OKAY, EMILY. HOW DO WE START?
WITH JET SKIS.

ARE YOU KIDDING?
NOPE! NOW LET'S GET CRACKIN'.

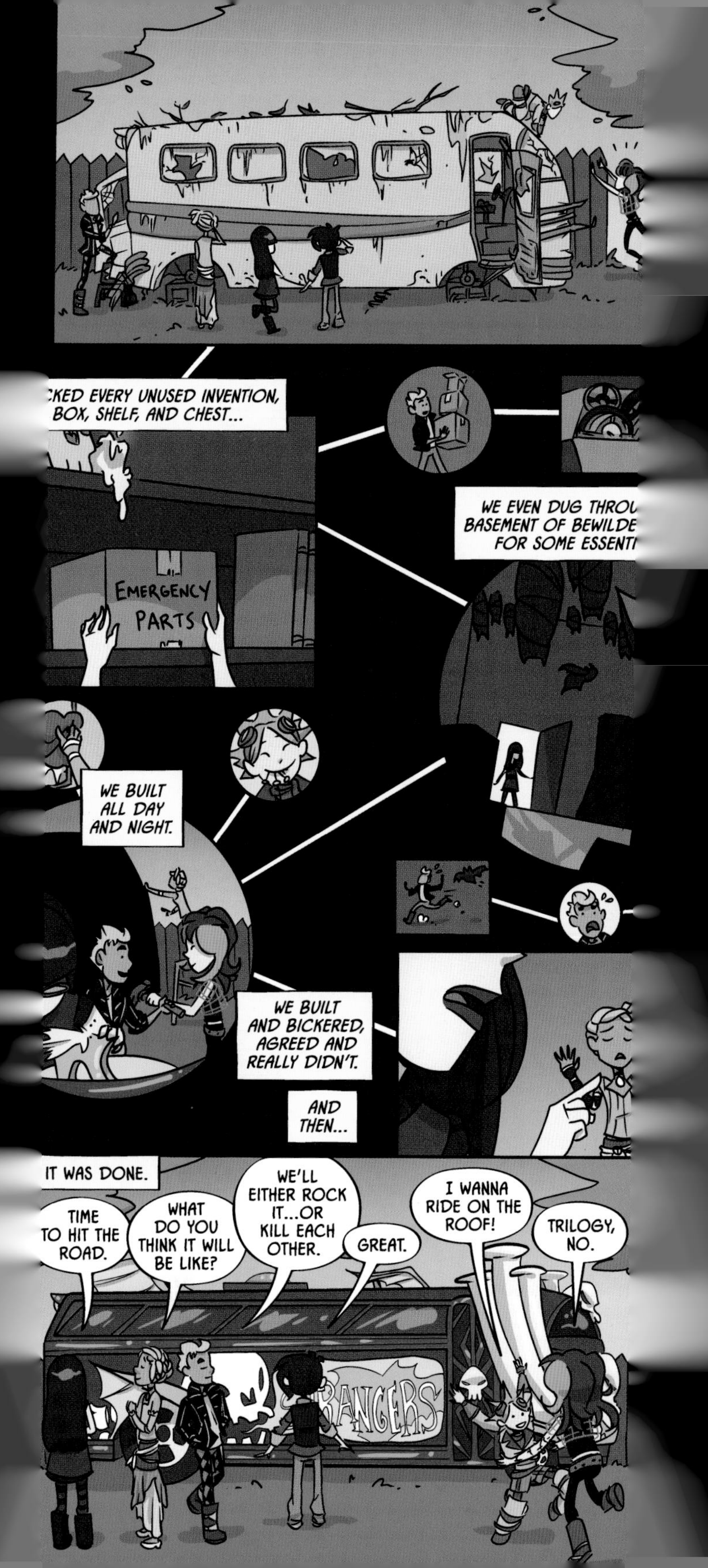
CKED EVERY UNUSED INVENTION, BOX, SHELF, AND CHEST...
EMERGENCY PARTS
WE EVEN DUG THROU BASEMENT OF BEWILDE FOR SOME ESSENTI
WE BUILT ALL DAY AND NIGHT.
WE BUILT AND BICKERED, AGREED AND REALLY DIDN'T.
AND THEN...
IT WAS DONE.
TIME TO HIT THE ROAD.
WHAT DO YOU THINK IT WILL BE LIKE?
WE'LL EITHER ROCK IT...OR KILL EACH OTHER.
GREAT.
I WANNA RIDE ON THE ROOF!
TRILOGY, NO.

EMILY AND THE STRANGERS
WE'VE GOT TO BE GOOD TONIGHT. NO FIGHTING!
I WON'T IF SHE WON'T.
HUSH UP, EV. WE SENT OUT THE EMAILS, GOT UP THE POSTERS. WE'RE GOLD.
EVERYONE ALREADY KNOWS WE ROCK. THEY'LL BE HERE.
CRAWLY DOESN'T KNOW WHO HE'S MESSING WITH.
I BET IT'S STANDING-ROOM ONLY. I BET IT'S--
NEARLY EMPTY?
DEADSVILLE?
ECHO!
WHAT IN THE HUCKBATS--
OH, NO.
CRAWLY GOT US.
KUTE WOW KITTIES POP-UP! TONIGHT!

THAT WAS EMBARRASSING. WE NEED TO SMASH THAT CRAWLING GUTTERFISHHEAD.
WE NEED A VIDEO. SOMETHING WE CAN GET OUT TO EVERYONE. LIKE HE DID. BUT BETTER.
A VIDEO? I DON'T KNOW...
ANYONE ELSE WONDERING WHY THAT FAN SHOWED US HER PHONE?
GINGERBREAD! HAVE TEA!
SHARK!
ISN'T THAT KIND OF...SELLOUTY? LIKE WE'RE MAKING OURSELVES INTO A COMMERCIAL?
NOT WHEN WE DO IT.
ER...
LOOK, IT'S EASY. WE'LL JUST HAVE ME ROCKING OUT WITH OUR SONGS, CATS EVERYWHERE, THEN I'LL TELL EVERYONE ABOUT CRAWLY.
ONCE EVERYONE SEES ME--
EMILY, THIS IS...JUST ***YOU.***
IT LOOKS LIKE YOU DON'T EVEN HAVE A ***BAND.***

SO?
WE'VE BEEN OVER THIS BEFORE. YOU CAN'T JUST TAKE OVER. THIS IS ABOUT MORE THAN ANY ONE OF US.
IT NEEDS TO BE ABOUT THE **CATS.** WHAT'S HAPPENING. WHY PEOPLE SHOULD HELP.
WE NEED PEOPLE TO LOVE THESE CATS. TO LOVE THEM NOT IN SPITE OF THEIR FLAWS...
...BUT ***BECAUSE*** OF THEM. THAT'S WHAT YOU TAUGHT US, EMILY.
WE NEED TO MAKE THEM CARE.
AND WE CAN'T DO THAT IF IT'S JUST YOU IN THE SPOTLIGHT. YOU NEED TO STEP BACK.
HE LIKES YOU.
THEY NEED HELP MORE THAN YOU NEED SOLO TIME.
I CAN NEVER TELL WHEN YOU'RE SERIOUS.
YOU'RE... RIGHT.
"WHAT."
"WOW."
"COOL!"
"BANANAS!"
MRRWR! PFFT! SSST! FWSSST!*
MOW!
*TRANSLATION: "GO ROUND UP SOME FRIENDS, AND HURRY!"

BROKEN, BREAKING, CRACKED...
YOU WERE THE PLANET AND I WAS A CAT...
NEVER CUTE, NEVER SWEET...
BUT WE ARE HERE JUST THE SAME...
AND WE'RE GONNA FIND THE BEAT...
AND YOU WILL NEVER BE THE SAME...
READY TO LAUNCH THE VIDEO?
READY.

HOW'S THE VID DOING? MORE HITS? IT'S BEEN TWO DAYS ALREADY.
NOT YET. IT CAN TAKE A--
VID TUBE
100
WHOA!
WHAT?
WE JUST WENT FROM LIKE ONE HUNDRED VIEWS TO OVER **TWO THOUSAND...** AND CLIMBING...
HOW?
UM... THAT OTHER BAND? THE COPY-CATS?
THEY KINDA... CALLED US OUT...
We'll out-wow Emily and the Strangers any day! Check out their lame home video!
THEY ARE GOING ***DOWN.***

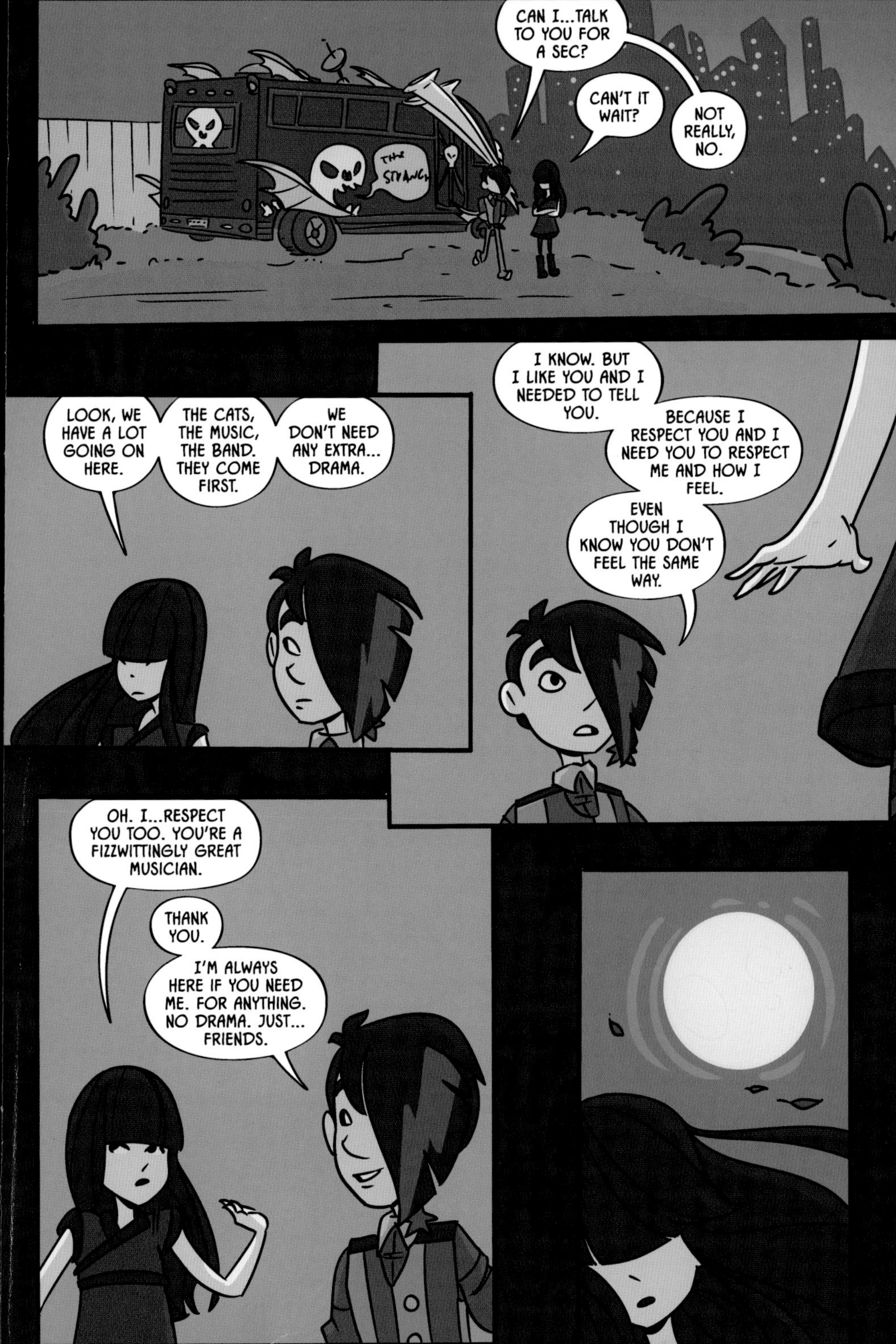
CAN I...TALK TO YOU FOR A SEC?
CAN'T IT WAIT?
NOT REALLY, NO.
LOOK, WE HAVE A LOT GOING ON HERE.
THE CATS, THE MUSIC, THE BAND. THEY COME FIRST.
WE DON'T NEED ANY EXTRA... DRAMA.
I KNOW. BUT I LIKE YOU AND I NEEDED TO TELL YOU.
BECAUSE I RESPECT YOU AND I NEED YOU TO RESPECT ME AND HOW I FEEL.
EVEN THOUGH I KNOW YOU DON'T FEEL THE SAME WAY.
OH. I...RESPECT YOU TOO. YOU'RE A FIZZWITTINGLY GREAT MUSICIAN.
THANK YOU.
I'M ALWAYS HERE IF YOU NEED ME. FOR ANYTHING. NO DRAMA. JUST... FRIENDS.

I GOT A NEW PLAN.
LET'S HEAR IT.
IT'S GOING TO SOUND WONKLEBEARS BUT--

WE'RE UP FOR IT.
ALWAYS.
WE NEED TO HELP THE KITTIES.
WE GOT YOUR BACK.
WHATEVER YOU NEED.
OKAY, THEN. HERE'S THE PLAN...

BIGGER! BRIGHTER! SPARE NO EXPENSE!
IT'S ALL ABOUT THE MUSIC, AFTER ALL!
MAKE SURE THE MERCH IS UP FRONT!
THESE ARE OUR RIVALS?
THEY LOOK LIKE A GARAGE BAND.
CRAWLY SAID IT'D BE A PIECE OF CAKE. THEY'RE IN ON THIS FAKE-CONTEST THING, ANYWAY. TO HELP US PROMOTE. CRAWLY SAID SO.
LIKE MY KUTE KITTIES?
HAND-PICKED THEM MYSELF. EAGER KIDS.
ALL THE BEST EQUIPMENT, SONGWRITERS, AND MUSIC WE COULD BUY.
YOU DON'T STAND A CHANCE.
WE ARE CUTE! WE ARE FINE! WE LOVE MUSIC AND HAVIN' A GOOD TIME!
ANIMALS ARE OUR FRIENDS! THEY'RE FLUFFY--THEY'RE FUN!
WE ARE CUTE! SO LET'S ROCK ON!
WE'RE UP. YOU SURE YOU CAN DO THIS?
I GOT THIS, EM.

STRANGERS.
NO PROBLEM.
WHAT ARE THEY DOING?
IT'S NOW OR NEVER. I HOPE I'M NOT MAKING A HUGE MISTAKE.
♫ DAMAGED GOODS--DRIFTING DOWN--WHERE DO WE GO WHEN THERE'S NOWHERE TO TURN...
♪ LOST, LOST, LOST--NO ONE TO FIND...

♫ HERE WE ARE AND THERE WE GO-- HOME WAS A MOMENT-- LOVE JUST A MOMENT-- AND NOW IT'S ALL GONE...
♪ GONE, HOME, GONE...
KUTE
WOW. WE DID IT.
TOGETHER.
YEAH.
DON'T GET EXCITED.
THAT WAS... WAS THAT FOR REAL?
CRAWLY TOLD US YOU GUYS WERE FAKES. A SETUP TO HELP US MAKE IT BIG.
HE'S A FLARFLEDRANNITY LYING LIAR. JUST LOOK AT HIS FAKE-O SMILE. AND ALL THOSE HAPPY CATS? MADE UP.
HE'S NOT A GOOD GUY. AND IT'S NOT JUST ABOUT THE MUSIC STUFF.
THAT'S REAL FOOTAGE FROM ONE OF THE AWESOMELY AWESOME FACTORIES.
THEY'RE SLAVES.
WE JUST WANTED TO PLAY. HE PROMISED US A LOT.
HE WON'T DELIVER.
THIS CALL-OUT CONCERT...IT WAS HIS IDEA. WE THOUGHT IT WAS JUST A FUN GIG.
YOU NEED TO MAKE A DECISION.
ARE YOU ABOUT THE MUSIC, OR ABOUT CRAWLY?
YOU WERE KINDA HARD ON THEM.
THEY NEEDED TO HEAR IT. LET'S GO. WE'VE GOT MORE WORK TO DO.

THE NEXT DAY, WE WERE READY FOR ANYTHING.
WHAT?! YOU CAN'T!
WE HAVE A CONTRACT!
YEAH, AND WE'RE DONE.
YOU LIED. THAT'S, LIKE... BREACH OR SOMETHING.
YOU'LL NEVER WORK IN THIS TOWN AGAIN!
CRAWLY
STUPID KIDS.
EVERYONE'S AGAINST ME. TRYING TO GET ONE OVER ON ME.
THOSE STRANGERS AND THEIR DO-GOODER MUSIC...
THEY ARE GONNA PAY...

CRAWLY WON'T LET THIS GO. WE HAVE TO BE PREPARED.
HOW DO WE PREDICT WHAT JERK INCORPORATED IS GOING TO DO?
HEY. WE CAME BY TO SAY--
IF IT'S ANYTHING OTHER THAN "WE QUIT THAT HUCKBAT CRAWLY," I'M NOT INTERESTED.
ACTUALLY, THAT'S EXACTLY WHAT WE DID. WE WANT TO HELP YOU GUYS SPREAD THE WORD ABOUT CRAWLY.
UH, THAT WAS QUICK...
HUH...
WOULD YOU GUYS LIKE SOME FOOD? WE'VE GOT LOTS.
YOU OKAY? CRAWLY CAN BE KINDA...MEAN WHEN HE DOESN'T GET WHAT HE WANTS.
THANKS, BUT WE NEED TO GET STARTED ON OUR OWN THING.
CRAWLY IS AWFUL BUT IF YOU CAN STAND UP TO HIM, WE CAN TOO.
WATCH OUT FOR CRAWLY. HE'S GUNNING FOR YOU GUYS.
ESPECIALLY YOU, EMILY.
LET 'IM JUST TRY SOMETHIN'.

YOU HEARD THEM. CRAWLY COULD TRY ANYTHING.
WE NEED TO TOUR HARD, FAST, AND TOUGH.
YEAH!
WE HIT THE DIY ZONE RUNNING.
DON'T EAT THAT!
SPARKLY!
YOU KNOW, IT REALLY HELPS TO HAVE A ROBOT GIRL IN YOUR BAND. SHE NEVER NEEDS SLEEP.
WHERE ARE WE HEADED NEXT?
SEND OUT THE EMAIL REMINDERS!
♫ ...AND KITTIES ARE JAMMING WITH SPACESHIPS...
CROOKED TAILS, HALF AN EAR, A LITTLE DAMAGED BUT STILL ROCKIN! ♪
THE STRANGERS

EVERY CITY WE COULD HIT, WE DID.
YOU DON'T HAVE TO BE CUTE TO BE AWESOME!
BIG CROWDS, LITTLE CROWDS, PARKS, PLAYHOUSES, AND CLUBS...
TONIGHT!
THE STRANGERS
I SANG UNTIL I WAS HOARSE.
HELP THE KITTIES!
THE STRANGERS
NOW IN DULLSVILLE!
ONE NIGHT ONLY
THE STRANGERS
STRANGE OUT!
THE BAND PLAYED UNTIL THEY WERE SORE.
WE DROVE ALL NIGHT AND DAY...
SPREADIN' THE WORD...

REMEMBER THE MUSIC...
REMEMBER THE BEAT...
THE KRAKEN
Prof. Kraken
WINSTON
EVAN
Willow
TRILOGY!
REMEMBER THE HEART OF THE SOUND...
RAVEN

YOU LOSE, EMILY...
YOU LOSE, YOU LOSE, YOU LOSE...
HA HA HA HA HA HA HA HA HA HA HA HA HA HA HA
HUCKAFARBOTTINGDRAPPLEBATS!
I NEED SOME AIR. NORMALLY I LIKE NIGHTMARES.
JAWS
I WISH THE PROFESSA WAS HERE...

EMILY? YOU OKAY?
YOU SEEM KIND OF... TIRED.
OF COURSE. JUST THINKIN'. ALONE.
I'M FINE, JUST...WISH IT WAS ALL EASIER.
I REALLY WANT TO HELP THOSE CATS, AND CRAWLY IS SUCH A--
EVIL ORANGE STICK?
SOMETHING LIKE THAT.

IT'S OKAY TO TELL PEOPLE YOU'RE TIRED, YOU KNOW. WE GET IT.
NOTED.
YEAH, WELL, TELL ANYONE ELSE AND YOU'LL LOSE A ***LIMB.***

THESE ARE SO... **MEAN.**
EM, YOU OKAY?
YEAH, IT'S JUST CRAWLY TRYIN' TO MAKE US LOOK--
--BAD?
AT AWESOMELY AWESOME INCORPORATED, ALL OUR SHELTERED ANIMALS ARE HAPPY AND CONTENT.
THE STRANGERS WERE A FAILED EXPERIMENT FROM OUR MUSIC DEPARTMENT.
THEY SIMPLY COULDN'T HANDLE THE WORK OF A BAND.
OR KEEPING THESE LITTLE GUYS HAPPY, OUR MOST IMPORTANT MESSAGE!
OH, IT IS **ON.**

SO, DO YOU THINK WE'LL BE ABLE TO CATCH WHOEVER IS--
SHHHH!
IT'S GOTTA BE HIM!
READY? LET'S--
CRUDLINS. WHERE IS CRAWLY?
WE'VE GOT A LITTLE MORE TIME BEFORE THE SHOW, EMILY.
I'M GETTING A CRICK IN THE CIRCUITS.
HE'S NOT SHOWING. BLARFBUGS.
DO YOU REALLY THINK CRAWLY IS DOING THIS BY HIMSELF NOW? SEEMS LIKE HE'D SEND OUT FLUNKIES OR SOMETHING.
NOW WHAT?
BEEP BOOP
WE HAVE TO GO PUBLIC. BUT WE NEED MY BOT'S INTEL FROM INSIDE AWESOMELY AWESOME.
IT'S GOT TO HAVE MEGA DIRT BY NOW.
I...DON'T KNOW.
BUT IT'S STILL INSIDE CRAWLY'S PLACE AND WE CAN'T REACH IT. HOW ARE WE GOING TO GET IT?

HM?
EMILY
slssh
RAVEN, I'M GOING OUT. TO THE OLD AWESOMELY AWESOME. DON'T TELL ANYONE UNLESS I DON'T COME BACK IN HALF AN HOUR.
TRILOGY! NO!
LET'S JUST GO BIG WITH WHAT WE KNOW.
CONTACT THE PRESS, EVERYONE...
BUT WE DON'T HAVE THE PROOF...
OKAY, THE NOTE SAID TO BE HERE ALONE AT EIGHT PM...HERE I AM.
OH, WINSTON... WHAT ARE YOU GETTING YOURSELF INTO...?
WHOA! I NEED TO GET EVERYONE HERE BEFORE--
PANEL ONE
OOOF!

WHERE'S WINSTON?
PROBABLY GOT HUNGRY. I'D CHECK BY THE SNACKS...
SPACE
BOY

WHAT IS THIS?
slshh

HE'S GOT WINSTON.
CRAWLY.
WHO?
GOT ONE OF YOUR PLAYERS. SHOW UP OR HE'LL BE SINGING A SAD TUNE!

THAT FARBOTTING GLARNOCK IS GOING DOWN.
EVERYTHING WE'VE GOT. NOW.

YOU GUYS WILL GO GET HIM-- USE RAVEN AND THE JET SKI/HOVER WINGS.
EVAN AND I WILL DISTRACT.
YOU GOT THIS?
GOT IT.

WHEN DID CRAWLY GRAB YOU?
JUST A LITTLE WHILE AGO. HE'S A SNAKE.
THESE POOR CATS. THEY DON'T KNOW WHAT THEY'RE *DOING...*

HEY, I KNOW THAT BOT...

I NEED THAT BOT. MAYBE IF I SING TO THEM...
♫ *CATS, CATS, WHISKERS AND BATS--HELP US HELP YOU BREAK OUT OF YOUR TRANCE--IT'S TIME TO GET GOING--IT'S TIME TO BE FREE--* ♪

IT WORKED!
NOW LET'S GET THAT BOT AND SEE IF WE CAN GET WHAT IT KNOWS TO EMILY...

WE NEED TO GET TO WINSTON AND THE BOT OR THIS WILL NEVER END. WE NEED TO FIGURE OUT EXACTLY WHERE THEY ARE.
I KNOW.
WINSTON IS MY PRIORITY. HE *HAS* TO BE.

HE'S EVERYONE'S.
WE WON'T LET YOU DOWN. WE'LL FIND HIM.
I PROMISE.

WHAT ABOUT THE CAT PROJECTOR?
IT REALLY CREEPS ME OUT WHEN YOU MAKE SENSE.
WHAT?
THE PROJECTOR WE USED TO FIND OUT WHAT THE KITTIES WERE AFRAID OF BY HEARING THEIR THOUGHTS.
WE CAN FIND WINSTON IF WE ADJUST IT TO SEARCH FOR HIS BRAIN WAVES.
THAT'S...A REALLY GOOD IDEA. WHY DIDN'T I THINK OF THAT?
HE'S LIKE A CAT ON THE INSIDE, ALL SOFT AND FLUFFY. AND HE SMELLS LIKE ORANGES AND SUMMER SUN.
HE'S SQUISHY!
YOU KNOW MY BROTHER PRETTY WELL.
AND THERE WE ARE, GOOD OLD RANDOM TRILOGY.
OKAY, THIS VID HAS TO BE PERFECT SO WE CAN INSERT THE BOT INFO AND GET IT OUT. FAST.
WE NEED TO MAKE SURE IT REACHES EVERYONE IT CAN, TOO.
EMAIL LIST? VIRAL VID? I'M ON IT.
YOU THINK EMILY AND TRILOGY CAN DO THIS?
I KNOW IT.
SHE DOESN'T SHOW IT, BUT EMILY CARES. A LOT. SHE WON'T STOP UNTIL WE GET HIM BACK.
DONE. YOU?
DITTO. LET'S RIDE.

WINNNSTONNN...
SORRY.
STOP THAT.
WINSTON? IT'S ME.

I THINK WE'RE...ALMOST THERE...

GOT HIM!
DRAPPLES.
WHAT IS IT? WE FOUND HIM... OH.

WILLOW?
ZZZWINSTON? ...ZZZ...WE'RE... COMING...
WAIT! DON'T!

ZZZZCAREFUL... CRAWLYZZZZ...
WE'RE GONNA NEED TO BREAK IN.

EVERYTHING HAS KEY CARDS AND CODES, EXCEPT THE LOADING DOCK.
BUT THAT HAS GUARDS 24/7.
GREAT, SO WHAT DO WE DO?
LIKE WILLOW SAID, WE NEED TO *FLY.*
MAP
NEWSTRINGS

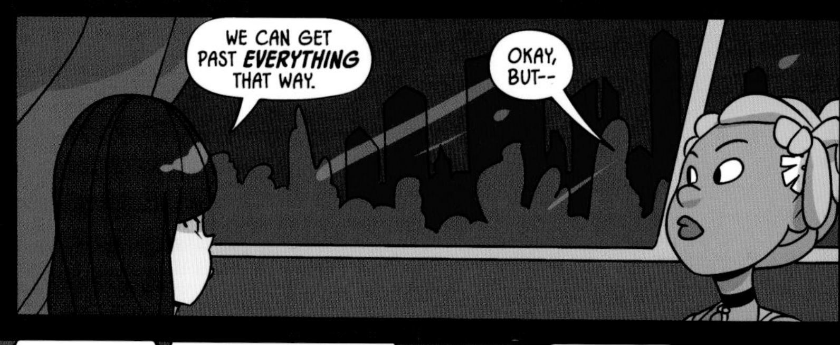
WE CAN GET PAST *EVERYTHING* THAT WAY.
OKAY, BUT--

WE STILL NEED A DISTRACTION. FOR CRAWLY. SOMEONE TO GET HIS ATTENTION.
WELL, SOMEONE COULD STAGE A PROTEST. GET THE PRESS. IT'LL BE DANGEROUS--CRAWLY COULD PULL SOMETHIN'...
ARE YOU SAYING YOU LIKE MY IDEA?
YEAH. DON'T LET IT GO TO YOUR HEAD.

SO WHO'S GONNA GO CONFRONT EVIL INCORPORATED DIRECTLY?
I'LL DISTRACT CRAWLY.
ARE YOU SURE? WE WON'T BE THERE TO HELP. YOU'LL BE ON YOUR OWN...

I'M GOING WITH YOU. TEAM DISTRACT, IN FULL FORCE.
I THOUGHT YOU MIGHT.

WE'LL HANDLE THE PEOPLE STUFF.
I THINK WE CAN MAKE CRAWLY... INTERESTED IN WHAT WE HAVE TO SAY.

GOT IT! LEARNED THAT TRICK FROM EMILY WHEN RAVEN HAD A SHORT.
YOU'RE A WEIRD BUNCH OF KIDS.
WILLOW? YOU HEAR ME? I'M UPLOADING FROM INSIDE. KEEP THE RECORDING SAFE.

JUST NEED THIS LITTLE GUY...

KITTY ARMY? LET'S GET OUT OF HERE!

I FEEL STUPID.
IT'S *CAMO.* NO ONE NOTICES CATS.
I'M A KITTY!
SCIENCE
HAMILTON

FREE THE CATS! TELL THE TRUTH!
AWESOMELY AWESOME ENSLAVES CATS!
MAKE CRAWLY CRAWL!
END CAT OPPRESSION

BOYCOTT AWESOMELY AWESOME!

STRANGERS! I ONLY SEE TWO OF YOU. WHAT'S ALL THIS?
ON SUCH A COLD NIGHT, TOO.
ROUGH TIME FOR A PROTEST.

WE READY?
YEP.
AYE AYE, CAPTAIN!

OOOH! SHINY! AND CHROME!
NOW, WE JUST NEED TO FIGURE OUT WHAT FLOOR--
BZZP! EMILY? IT'S WINSTON! GO UP! UP!
WE KNOW! BUT WHERE?
TWENTIETH FLOOR! NEAR CRAWLY'S OFFICE! CAN'T MISS IT!

HOLD ON!
WHHHEEEE!
RADICAL DRADICAL.

HEY, DOCTOR CAT LADY, YAY!
WHERE'S WINSTON?
HE'S--
ZZZZZRAVEN! **EMILY!** THESE CATS NEED OUT **NOW!** IT'S A FULL-ON **STAMPEDE** IN HERE!

HI, EVERYONE! HAVE SOME HOT COCOA ON AWESOMELY AWESOME!
TELL THEM WHAT YOU DID.
I HAVE NO IDEA WHAT YOU MEAN, YOUNG MAN.
AWESOMELY AWESOME ENSLAVES CATS!
END CAT OPPRESSION
TELL THEM WHAT YOU DO TO THESE CATS.
HOW YOU THREATEN PEOPLE WHO DON'T DO WHAT YOU WANT.
THREATS? OH DEAR, I THINK WE'VE HAD A MISUNDERSTANDING.
BUT BY ALL MEANS, COME INSIDE! WE'RE AN OPEN BOOK.

YOU TWO DON'T KNOW WHO YOU'RE MESSING WITH.

SURE THING, MR. CRAWLY.
JUST SHOW US AND, IF THERE REALLY IS NOTHING GOING ON HERE, WE'LL GO AWAY.

FINALLY! WHAT'D YOU GUYS DO, STOP FOR A SNACK?
WATCH IT, PUNK.
SQUISHY FRIEND!
SEE?
Kute Kut
KUTE KITTY P
THIS IS HORRIBLE.
HOW CAN THEY...
WORKER DRONES. JUST TO MAKE AWESOMELY AWESOME STUFF.
I KNOW. THEY'RE SO UNHAPPY. THEY DON'T WANT TO BE DOING THIS.
602
KITTIES! THEY NEED TO BE FREE! HE'S SUFFOCATING THEIR MINDS!
WHERE IS THAT CRAWLY? I'M GOING TO SCREAM AT HIM UNTIL HE MELTS!
IT'S OKAY, TRIL. WE'RE GOING TO FIX IT.
DEFINITELY.
WE NEED TO GET THEM OUT OF HERE, EMILY.
YES. WE DO. BUT...

...BUT WE ALSO NEED TO MAKE SURE THEY KNOW WHERE THEY GO. AND THAT EVERYONE KNOWS OR CRAWLY WILL KEEP DOING THIS.
I'VE GOT TO THINK.

WOULD THIS HELP?
YOU FOUND IT!

WOW.

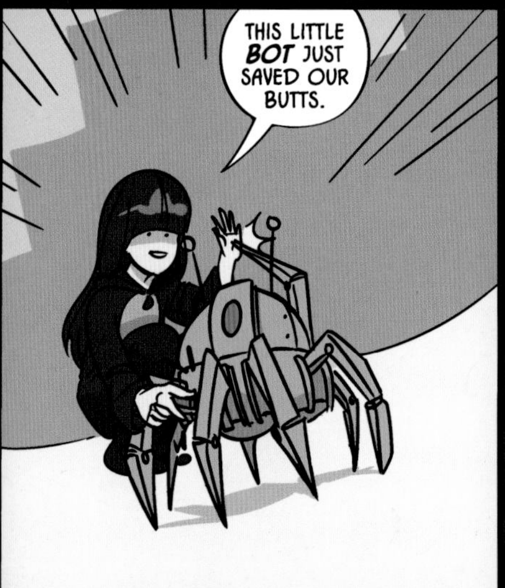
THIS LITTLE **BOT** JUST SAVED OUR BUTTS.

WINSTON? I THINK I KNOW WHAT TO DO--

AS YOU CAN SEE, IT'S ALL STATE OF THE ART, EVERYTHING NEW AND MODERN.
AND NOT A CAT IN SIGHT.
YOU KNOW THE INTERNET THESE DAYS, ONE PERSON SAYS SOMETHING AND THEN PEOPLE BELIEVE IT...
WE EVEN HAVE A CHARITY FOR ABANDONED ANIMALS.

WHO WANTS A SMOOTHIE? ORGANIC!

I HOPE EMILY AND THE OTHERS GOT WHAT WE NEED.
ME TOO.

THEY GOT CAUGHT?
I CAN'T SEE EMILY LETTING THAT HAPPEN, CAN YOU?
NO, BUT--
WHAT THE--

UM, EV?
WHOA.
NOW IF EVERYONE WOULD JUST--
RROOOOWWR

HSSSSS
ROWWWR
FIZZZZZ
DUMB
NO! I'M ALLERGIC!

HEY, CRAWLY. GUESS WHAT WE FOUND?
I'LL JUST HIT PLAY AND THEN EVERYONE WILL KNOW--
CRACK

HA, HA! NOW YOU HAVE NOTHING!
IT WAS ALL FOR NOTHING!
NO...
I'M JUST GLAD YOU'RE SAFE...
NOTHING? WELL--

RAVEN'S GOT IT ALL. THAT'S ONE OF THE MANY ADVANTAGES TO HAVING A ROBOT GIRL FOR A FRIEND.
SHE CAN DOWNLOAD **ANYTHING.**

I THINK THIS IS WHAT WE CALL... **OWNED?**

I'M RUINED.

I TOLD YOU. DON'T MESS WITH EMILY OR--

MY **FRIENDS.**

CRAWLY'S LIFE WAS GONNA BE PRETTY TERRIBLE FROM HERE ON IN.

NOT EVEN REMOTELY SORRY ABOUT THAT.

AND WE HAD A WHOLE OTHER PROBLEM NOW ANYWAY.

WE NEED A BIGGER HOUSE.
I DON'T THINK ANY HOUSE CAN CONTAIN ALL THESE KITTIES.

EVERYONE KNOWS NOW, BUT THESE CATS STILL NEED HOMES.
WE NEED TO DO RIGHT BY THEM.

IT'S TOO MANY CATS EVEN FOR ME.
WE NEED A SOLUTION.

TAKE THEM TO LOCAL SHELTERS?
THERE'S TOO MANY.
SET UP AN ADOPTION HERE?
THEN WE'RE STILL DROWNING IN CATS.

WE NEED TO DO CONCERTS WITH ADOPTIONS. AND THEN OPEN OUR OWN SHELTER!
SERIOUSLY NOW, ANYONE ELSE WEIRDED OUT BY HER LUCIDITY BURSTS?

HOW ABOUT A FAIR, TOO? LIKE, FOR CATS AND MUSIC AND EVERYTHING AWESOME?

NAILED IT. WAY TO GO, TRILOGY.
SERIOUSLY, THIS IDEA IS PERFECT.
NOW PLAY SOMETHING ORANGE!

FREE CATS! FREE MUSIC! BRING A WEIRDLY WONDERFUL CAT HOME!
WEIRD CATS ARE WONDERFUL FAIR
CATS MAKE YOU HAPPY! IT'S SCIENCE!

THESE CATS ARE ONE OF A KIND.
JUST LIKE YOU.
MY CAT, GINGERBREAD, MAKES ME SANDWICHES WHEN I FEEL WOOGY.
THEY CUDDLE WHEN YOU'RE SICK, SLEEP WITH YOU...

HIS NAME IS WRINKLES, AND EVEN THOUGH HE LOOKS TOUGH...

REALLY, HE'S THE ***SWEETEST.***

WE COMPOSE TOGETHER EVEN THOUGH HE'S DEAF.
I NAMED HIM MOZART.
JUNIPER IS BLIND BUT SHE'S THE CUDDLIEST.
AND CRACKERS MAY HAVE THREE LEGS, BUT HE LOVES TO JUMP!
YOU'RE GOING TO LOVE ANGEL, MRS. PICKLE. HE'S A TOTAL LAP CAT.
YOUR TWINS ARE GOING TO HAVE SUCH A GREAT TIME WITH NOODLES. SHE'S OLDER AND KNOWS HOW TO HANDLE KIDS.
WE'LL MISS YOU, NOODLES, BUT THESE FOLKS ARE THE BEST.
MEOW!
THE FIX
HOT DOGS
THERE OUGHTA BE A SLAW!

CARING FOR OTHER CREATURES IS THE BEST THING I'VE EVER DONE.
EVERYONE NEEDS SOMEONE TO LOVE.
I ATTRACT ALL KINDS!
ONE, TWO, READY-- *CRAZY KITTY TIME!*

WHERE'S EMILY?
DOING HER OWN THING. BEHIND THE SCENES THIS TIME.

HEY. IT'S GOING REALLY WELL OUT THERE.
WANT TO COME CHEC IT OUT?
GOOD. CATS NEED IT.

NAH. I'M NOT INTO THE PEOPLE THING.
I WAS THINKING MAYBE IT'S TIME FOR ME TO, YOU KNOW...
MOVE ON. RAVEN AND WINSTON AND TRILOGY HAVE THIS, AND I MISS MY STUDIO.

WHATEVER. DO YOUR THING.
OH.

I GUESS I'LL SEE YOU... LATER.

WHAT THE HUCKBATS WAS THAT?
WHAT? HE WANTS OUT. I CAN SEE THE WRITING ON THE WALL.
I DON'T NEED HIM.
YOU KNOW, IF AFTER EVERYTHING, YOU STILL CAN'T MANAGE TO CARE ABOUT A FRIEND'S FEELINGS...
THEN I'M NOT SURE WE CAN BE FRIENDS, EITHER.
WILLOW...
I'M SERIOUS. DO YOU CARE WHAT I THINK?
...YES.
THEN FIX IT. GO AFTER HIM.
STUPID FEELINGS.
STUPID BOYS.
STUPID DOING THE RIGHT THING.
STUPID EVAN BEING HARD TO FIND.

WEIRD CAT FAIR
FINALLY.
EVAN, CAN WE... TALK?
AS LONG AS BY "TALK" YOU DON'T MEAN YELL A LOT AND INSULT ME.

LOOK, I HATE THIS MUSHY STUFF, BUT...YOU'RE MY FRIEND.
AND I DON'T WANT THAT TO STOP.
SO... STOP BEING A PILL AND STICK AROUND. LET'S JAM SOMETIME.

THANK YOU, EMILY.
URK.

OKAY, DON'T YOU **EVER** DO THAT AGAIN.
WEIRD
NOTED.

NOW THAT IT'S ALL DONE, IT FEELS... WEIRD.

SOOO... NOW WHAT?
GOOD QUESTION.

DOWN AT THE SHELTER, THERE ARE STILL SO MANY CATS WHO NEED GOOD HOMES.
PEOPLE SEEM TO REALLY TRUST ME, THOUGH.
I REALLY LOVE HELPING OUT. I WAS THINKING I COULD BE A VET...
I SEEM TO BE PRETTY GOOD AT ROUNDING UP WEIRD CRITTERS.

I WANT PIE! WITH *BERRIES!*
I WAS THINKING ABOUT, MAYBE, YOU KNOW, TRYING SOME SONGS OUT ON MY OWN...

IT'S REALLY ENDING, ISN'T IT? THE BAND?
WELL, WE'VE ALL GOT OTHER THINGS GOING ON, YOU KNOW?
WE CAN'T BE TOGETHER *ALL* THE TIME.

BUT WE'LL STAY IN TOUCH. RIGHT, EMILY?

I HATE OWING ANYONE.
AND I NEVER WANTED A BAND.
BUT NOW THAT I HAVE ONE, NOW THAT I KNOW YOU AND HAVE WORKED WITH YOU ON SO MUCH...
I DON'T WANT IT TO END, EITHER.

IT SOUNDS CHEESY, BUT WE WEREN'T STRANGERS ANYMORE.
WE'D COME A LONG WAY.
THE STRANGERS

BUT EVEN
GOOD THINGS
HAVE TO END.
AND IF YOU
CAN GO OUT WITH
A LITERAL BANG?

AFTER THAT, EVERYONE KIND OF FOUND THEIR OWN GROOVE.
SIX MORE ADOPTIONS TODAY, ALL GREAT HOMES.
I MADE PICTURES!
GO ON AND PUT THEM UP ON THE SUCCESS WALL OF FAME.
ADOPT A CAT
I STARTED THIS PROGRAM THAT TAKES MY PIANO RIFFS AND TURNS THEM INTO VOICES...
♫ MY NAME IS FULL OF ROOTS, THOSE ROOTS GO DEEP, AND WHEN I BLOSSOM, JUST YOU WAIT AND SEE... ♪
WE DID GOOD.
WHEN SHALL WE SIX MEET AGAIN?
WE SHOULD KEEP A REGULAR DATE. OR DATES.
YEAH, WE'LL ***ALWAYS*** NEED TO JAM.
AND CHECK IN.
YEAH. WE WILL.

AND THEN IT WAS QUIET.
WHICH I USED TO THINK WAS ALL I NEEDED.
NOT ANYMORE.
WILLOW LIKES SOME WEIRD STUFF, BUT IT'S OKAY.
AND I HAVE TO ADMIT, OOLONG TEA IS PRETTY GOOD.
WE HANG ONCE A WEEK, MORE THAN ANYONE ELSE.

RAVEN AND I STILL LISTEN TO RECORDS LIKE THE OLD DAYS.
SHE SAYS THE SHELTER IS THE BEST TIME SHE'S EVER HAD.
DOOMTREE

PIP
WHEN I NEED 'EM, THEY'RE ALWAYS THERE.

I EVEN JAM WITH EVAN.

TRILOGY AND I HAVE AN INTERESTING RELATIONSHIP.
I STILL HAVE NO IDEA WHAT MAKES HER TICK.

AND I KNOW THINGS ARE ALWAYS GOING TO BE INTERESTIN' AND FUN AND WEIRD.
BECAUSE...I'VE GOT FRIENDS.
AND THEY ROCK.
THE END

Emily® and the Strangers

SKETCHBOOK

ART BY
CAT FARRIS
and **BUZZ PARKER**

Some of Cat's sketches for
Emily and the gang.

On the next pages are some of her layouts and inks.
See the final versions on pages 39 and 68 of this book!

A
CAT

ADOPT A CAT

A
Emily the Strange
Strangers

B
Emily the Strange
GET LOST!

C
Emily the Strange
STRANE

D
Emily the Strange

Buzz's sketch ideas for the cover (*facing*) and his two penciled versions before moving on to inks (*this page*).

EMILYSTRANGE.COM
ALL THESE ITEMS AVAILABLE NOW
MARKET PLACE

The ART of Emily the Strange

NEW BOOK
AVAILABLE NOW!
200 PAGES!
OF STRANGE!

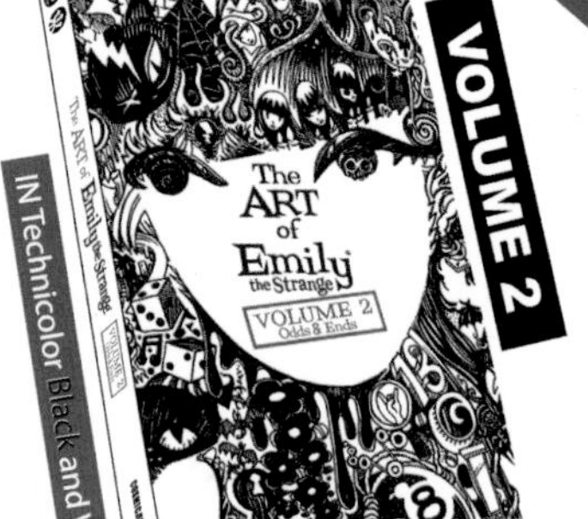

"The GREATEST Strange Book of all time..."
- Hieronymus Bosch

EmilyStrangerous
the Art of Emily the Strange

ETSY.COM/SHOP/EMILYSTRANGEROUS

Original Artwork
SKETCHES PAINTINGS INK DRAWINGS
Limited Edition Art Prints

DESIGNER JEWELRY

Emily® the Strange

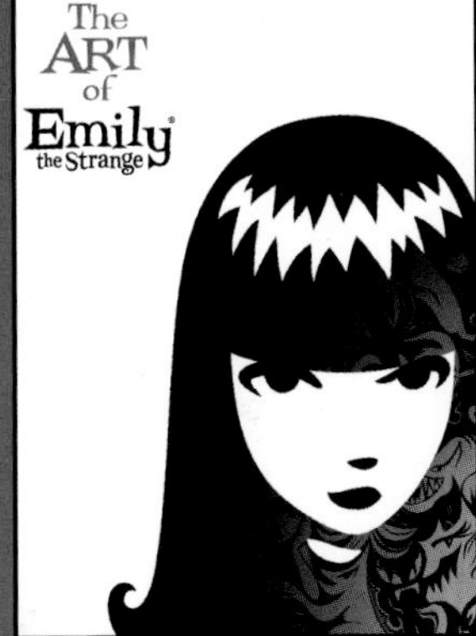

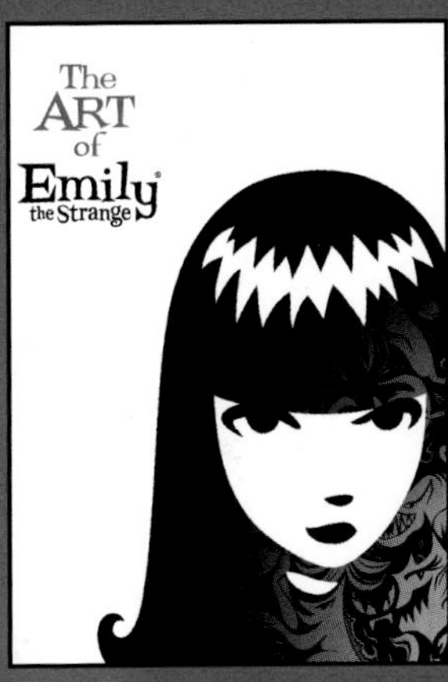

Strange books for strange readers!

THE COMPLETE EMILY THE STRANGE: ALL THINGS STRANGE
ISBN 978-1-50670-061-8 | $19.99

EMILY AND THE STRANGERS VOLUME 1: THE BATTLE OF THE BANDS
ISBN 978-1-61655-323-4 | $12.99

EMILY AND THE STRANGERS VOLUME 2: BREAKING THE RECORD
ISBN 978-1-61655-598-6 | $12.99

EMILY AND THE STRANGERS VOLUME 3: ROAD TO NOWHERE TOUR
ISBN 978-1-50670-058-8 | $12.99

THE ART OF EMILY THE STRANGE
ISBN 978-1-59582-371-7 | $22.99